interchange

English for international communication

Jack C. Richards

with Jonathan Hull
and Susan Proctor

1

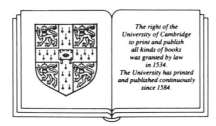

*The right of the
University of Cambridge
to print and publish
all kinds of books
was granted by law
in 1534.
The University has printed
and published continuously
since 1584.*

Workbook

Cambridge University Press

Cambridge • **New York** • **Port Chester** • **Melbourne** • **Sydney**

Published by the Press Syndicate of the University of Cambridge
The Pitt Building, Trumpington Street, Cambridge CB2 1RP
40 West 20th Street, New York, NY 10011, USA
10 Stamford Road, Oakleigh, Melbourne 3166, Australia

© Cambridge University Press 1990

First published 1990
Second printing 1990

Printed in the United States of America

ISBN 0 521 35990 2 Workbook One
ISBN 0 521 35988 0 Student's Book One
ISBN 0 521 35989 9 Teacher's Manual One
ISBN 0 521 35203 7 Class Cassette Set One
ISBN 0 521 35204 5 Student Cassette One

Book design: Circa 86, Inc.
Cover design: Tom Wharton

Illustrators
Jack DeGraffenried
David Jarvis
Bill Thomson

Contents

Acknowledgments

Illustrators
Jack DeGraffenried 1, 2, 4, 7, 10, 11, 12, 13, 14, 34 (bottom), 35, 36, 38 (top and middle), 50
David Jarvis 21, 33, 34 (top), 47, 54
Bill Thomson 6, 22, 37, 38 (bottom), 39, 45, 46, 57

Photographic Credits
The authors and publishers are grateful for permission to reproduce the following photographs. Every endeavor has been made to contact copyright owners, and apologies are expressed for omissions.

1 © John Terence Turner/FPG International

5 *(a)* © Jeffry W. Myers/FPG International; *(b)* Copyright © 1985 Marc P. Anderson. All rights reserved; *(c)* Shostal Associates/SuperStock International, Inc.; *(d)* Copyright © 1985 Marc P. Anderson. All rights reserved.

6 *(a)* © Shelley Gazin/The Image Works; *(b)* Scott Dornblaser (Biomedical Photography TAH-LVHC)/Allentown Hospital, Allentown, Pa.; *(c)* © Catherine Ursillo/Photo Researchers, Inc.; *(d)* © Jeffry W. Myers/FPG International

9 SuperStock International, Inc.

14 *(left to right)* Globe Photos, Inc.; Kobal Collection/SuperStock International, Inc.; © J. Zerschling/Photo Researchers, Inc.; © Tim Ryan/Gamma-Liaison

17 *(top)* © Arvind Garg 1989; *(center)* © David Wells/The Image Works; *(bottom)* © FourByFive/SuperStock International, Inc.

18 *(clockwise from upper left)* Oscar Abolafia/Gamma-Liaison; Kobal Collection/SuperStock International, Inc.; Sylvia Norris/Globe Photos, Inc.; LucasFilm/Kobal Collection/SuperStock International, Inc.

19 Mark Antman/The Image Works

20 *(a)* © George Gardner/The Image Works; *(b)* © Arvind Garg 1989; *(c)* © Arvind Garg 1989; *(d)* © FourByFive/SuperStock International, Inc.; *(e)* Copyright © 1985 Marc P. Anderson. All rights reserved; *(f)* © Helen Marcus 1982/Photo Researchers, Inc.

23 *(left to right)* Copyright © 1980 Marc P. Anderson. All rights reserved; © Dion Ogust/The Image Works; © Charles Gatewood/The Image Works

25 © Wendell D. Metzen/Bruce Coleman, Inc., New York

26 *(both)* © Tourespaña, Madrid

27 *(a)* © Tom McHugh. All rights reserved/Photo Researchers, Inc.; *(b)* © James Blank/Stock, Boston

31 © L. H. Mangino/The Image Works

41 *(top)* Grant Heilman, Lititz, Pa.; *(bottom)* Copyright 1989, Comstock

42 *(left)* Schuster/SuperStock International, Inc.; *(right)* The Photo Source/SuperStock International, Inc.

43 *(above)* © MCMLXXVI Peter Menzel/Stock, Boston; *(below)* © Bohdan Hrynewych/Stock, Boston

44 *(left)* © Fritz Henle 1972/Photo Researchers, Inc.; *(right)* © LXXXIV Gary Crallé/The Image Bank

46 R. Pleasant/FPG International

49 L.O.L., Inc./FPG International

51 © FourByFive/SuperStock International, Inc.

53 *(above)* © Arvind Garg 1989; *(below)* Kenneth C. Poertner, Boise, Idaho

55 *(top)* Len Rue, Jr./FPG International; *(bottom left)* Courtesy Australian Tourist Commission, New York; *(bottom center)* Copyright Stuart Cohen/Copyright 1988, Comstock; *(bottom right)* Courtesy Swiss National Tourist Office, New York

60 *(both)* Courtesy Central Cellular Company, Chicago

1 Please call me Dave

1 Write about yourself.

My first name is ....

My last name is ....

Please call me ....

I am from .... (city).

I am .... (nationality).

I am a/an .... (job).

2 Names

1 Write **M** for male names and **F** for female names.

a) _F_ Margaret   f) .... David

b) .... James   g) .... Robert

c) .... Catherine   h) .... Susan

d) .... Michael   i) .... Thomas

e) .... Elizabeth   j) .... Jennifer

2 Now match each of these short names with a name above.

Bob   Cathy   Jenny   Dave   Jim   Liz   Maggie   Mike   Sue   Tom

....   _a._   ....

3 Match the following.

a)   a full name with a title   ....   _Michael Charles Kennedy_

b)   a short name   ....   _P. W. C._

c)   a full name without a title   ....   _Smith_

d)   a family name   ....   _Cathy_

e)   initials   ....   _Ms. Celia Frances Jones_

1

4 **Complete the conversation with these words:**

a   am   an   are   do   from   is

A: Hi! I .... Jack Jones. What .... your name?

B: I .... Marie.

A: And what .... your last name?

B: My last name .... Dupont.

A: Are you .... the United States, Marie?

B: No, I .... from Canada.

A: Oh? What city .... you from?

B: I .... from Montreal.

A: Really? What do you .... ?

B: I'm .... journalist. How about you?

A: I'm .... engineer.

5 **Match the sentences in A and B to make a conversation.**

A

a) I'm Ken Morita.

b) Nice to meet you, too. Sorry.
    How do you say your name again?

c) Where are you from, Jane?

d) Really? And are you studying there?

e) I'm a student. I'm studying computer
    science.

B

.... No, I'm not. I'm a high school teacher.
And how about you?

.... Oh, really? How interesting!

.... I'm Jane Thomas. Nice to meet you.

.... It's Thomas. Jane Thomas.

.... Washington. But I live in Toronto now.

6 **Find the names of six jobs.**

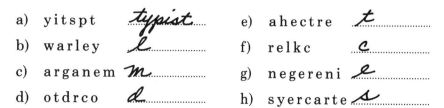

a) y i t s p t   *typist*

b) w a r l e y   *l*

c) a r g a n e m   *m*

d) o t d r c o   *d*

e) a h e c t r e   *t*

f) r e l k c   *c*

g) n e g e r e n i   *e*

h) s y e r c a r t e   *s*

7 **Look at the answers. What are the questions?**

a) What ....? My first name's Bob.

b) What ....? My last name's Hayes.

c) How ....? H-A-Y-E-S.

d) What ....? I'm a sales manager.

e) Where ....? My wife is from Mexico.

f) What ....? Her name is Rosa.

8 **Circle the correct word.**

a) They're my classmates. (They/Their) names are Noriko and Vera.

b) We live in the dormitory. (Our/We) room number is 108-C.

c) Excuse me. What's (you/your) last name again?

d) That's Mr. de Souza. (He/His) is in my class.

e) Please call (me/my) Liz.

f) That's Paul's wife. (His/Her) name is Francine.

9 **Where are these countries?**

1 Write **A** for Asia, **AF** for Africa, **E** for Europe, **ME** for Middle East, and **SA** for South America. More than one answer is possible.

.... Brazil .... France .... Kenya .... Peru .... Taiwan

.... Chile .... Italy .... Korea .... Portugal .... Turkey

.... China .... Japan .... Kuwait .... Saudi Arabia

.... Egypt .... Jordan .... Nigeria .... Spain

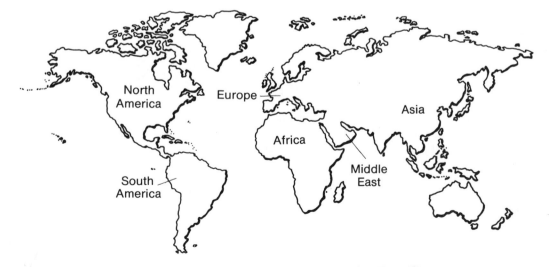

2 What is the nationality for each country? For example, Brazil – Brazilian.

---

10 **Look at the answers. What are the questions?**

a) Are .... ?
   No, I'm not on vacation. I'm a student.

b) .... ?
   No, I'm not from Spain. I'm from Mexico.

c) .... ?
   Yes, I'm staying in a dormitory – the women's dorm on campus.

d) .... ?
   No, I'm not in English 101. I'm in English 102.

e) .... ?
   No, my teacher isn't Mr. Brown. I'm in Ms. West's class.

f) .... ?
   Yes, Ms. West is Australian.

---

11 **Choose the correct response.**

a) Good morning, Dave.   .... Oh, hello.
                                .... See you later.

b) Have a nice evening.   .... Yes, it is.
                                .... Thanks. You, too. Bye!

c) Excuse me. Are you Jim Hall? .... Please call me John.
                                .... Yes, I am.

d) See you on Monday.   .... Thanks. You, too!
                                .... OK. See you.

e) By the way, what do you do?   .... I'm a student.
                                .... Yes, I'm a homemaker.

2 It's a great job!

1 **Read the job descriptions and find the correct job.**

cook   photographer   salesperson   typist
factory worker reporter   supervisor   waitress

a) I work in a department store.
    I sell jewelry.

    I'm a ....

b) I work in a restaurant.
    I serve the meals.

    I'm a ....

c) I work for a TV station.
    I report on people in the news.

    I'm a ....

d) I work for a clothing company.
    I make shirts and suits.

    I'm a ....

2 **Pronunciation: Underline the stressed syllable in each word.**

afternoon	college	hotel	photographer	sixteen
apartment	department	Japanese	receptionist	tomorrow
Argentina	factory	Monday	seventy	Wednesday

3 Complete the questions in this conversation.

A: Where ....?
B: I work for American Express.

A: What .... there?
B: I'm in the accounting department.

A: Where ....?

B: I live downtown near my office. And what ....
....?

A: I'm a graduate student in engineering.

B: Where .... school?
A: I go to Cal State. Also, I'm a part-time salesclerk.

B: Really? What ....?
A: I sell Apple computers. Do you want to buy one?

---

4 What a job!

1 The article **a** or **an** is missing from each sentence in these descriptions. Write **a** or **an** in the correct place.

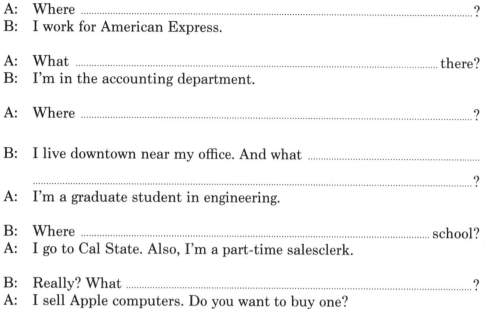

a) I'm *a* driver. I work for travel company. I drive bus, and I take people on tours.

b) I'm nurse. I work in public hospital. I have interesting job.

c) I'm waitress. I work in Italian restaurant. I'm also taking English course at night.

d) I'm counselor. I work in elementary school. It's great job.

2 What do you do? Now write about yourself.

5 Choose the correct preposition.

A: Do you still work .... (for/to) the bus company?

B: No. I work .... (to/at) Macy's now. I work .... (from/in) the toy department.

A: I hate my job! I work .... (for/at) the government. I'm .... (in/for) the tax department. It's really boring. How about you?

B: Oh, I work .... (from/in) a gym downtown. I teach aerobics. Come by sometime!

A: Do you work .... (in/to) a high school?

B: No, I work .... (from/at) Honolulu Community College. I teach .... (in/from) the sports department. I teach surfing from nine to five .... (to/at) the beach. It's a tough job.

A: Where do you go .... (at/to) school?

B: I'm studying .... (for/at) City College. I'm .... (in/on) the Asian languages department. I'm majoring .... (in/with) Japanese.

6 Choose the correct response.

a) Thank you very much.

.... You're welcome.
.... That's right.

b) How's everything?

.... Pretty good, thanks.
.... Yes, it is, thanks.

c) I work for the French embassy.

.... That looks interesting.
.... That sounds interesting.

d) I work in Japan now.

.... Oh, really?
.... Oh, are you?

e) Is your phone number 874-3215?

.... That's right.
.... No, thanks.

7 Crossword puzzle: Verbs

Use these verbs to complete the crossword puzzle.

get	serve	study	use
go	sell	take	work
help	start	type	write

Across clues

1 I .... work at 6 o'clock
   in the morning.
5 I .... in an office downtown.
6 Where can you .... the number 13 bus?
7 Where do you .... computer science?
9 They .... good food in our
   company cafeteria.
10 Flight attendants .... passengers
   on a plane.

Down clues

2 I .... the subway to work.
3 I .... all my letters on a computer.
4 I .... home in a friend's car
   after work.
5 I .... about five letters a week.
7 We .... imported cars in our showroom.
8 We .... Spanish and English
   in our office.

8 Fill in the missing words in these job ads.

| appointment | majoring | free | afternoons | good | full-time |
| part-time | necessary | needed | salary | company | interviews |

Lab technician. ....
job for college student
.... in science.
$6.50 an hour. Start in
July. No experience
.... Call Dr.
Ladd at 879-1005 for an
....

Food and beverage
manager .... for
Mexican restaurant. Work
.... and
evenings. ....
meals and good
.... 872-9135.

.... salesperson
wanted for telephone
....
.... English and
Spanish needed.
.... Wednesday,
Sept. 23, 9–noon, 321 First
St.

3 I'm just looking, thanks

1 How much is it?

1 Write the numbers for these prices.

$ *3,010*   three thousand and ten dollars

£ ....   six hundred and seventy-two pounds

F ....   one thousand one hundred and ninety-nine francs

Ptas ....   two million forty-eight thousand pesetas

¥ ....   fifteen thousand seven hundred and fifty yen

2 Write out these prices in words.

$181 *a hundred (and) eighty-one dollars*

£519 ....

F114,067 ....

Ptas1,089 ....

¥12,300 ....

2 Expenses

1 How much do these things cost in your city?

A haircut costs about ....

A cup of coffee is ....

A good pair of jeans costs ....

2 Now write about the cost of five other things in your city.

PSYCHIATRIC
HELP 5¢

THE DOCTOR
IS [IN]

© 1950, 1952 United Feature Syndicate, Inc.

3 **Circle the word that does not belong in each list.**

a) blouse   bracelet   jacket   trousers

b) boots   sandals   shorts   slippers

c) road   motorcycle   truck   van

d) bookcase   briefcase   cupboard   desk

e) calculator   computer   notebook   typewriter

4 **Choose the correct pronoun.**

A: Excuse me, Mary.

    Are these socks (your/yours)?

B: No, those are not (my/mine).

    (My/Mine) socks are red.

A: I think that's (Jane/Jane's) new racquet.

B: No, that's not (her/hers).

A: Is this Pat (Hill/Hill's) watch?

B: No, it's not (her/hers).

A: Betty and Jean, are these (your/yours) bags?

B: Yes, those are (our/ours).

5 **Spelling check**

Plural Nouns	
Add **-s**	bag – bags
Drop y and add **-ies**	factory – factories
Add **-s** or **-es**	college – colleges
	glass – glasses

" I MISS THE GOOD OLD DAYS WHEN ALL WE HAD TO WORRY ABOUT WAS NOUNS AND VERBS."

© 1990 by Sidney Harris

Write the plurals of these words.

a) bank ....

b) bus ....

c) city ....

d) clerk ....

e) house ....

f) dish ....

g) office ....

h) secretary ....

i) shirt ....

j) shoe ....

k) sweater ....

l) tax ....

6 Pronunciation

Put the plural nouns in Exercise 5 into three lists.

Words ending with /z/   *Words ending with /s/*   *Words ending with /ɪz/*

                            banks

7 Circle the correct pronoun.

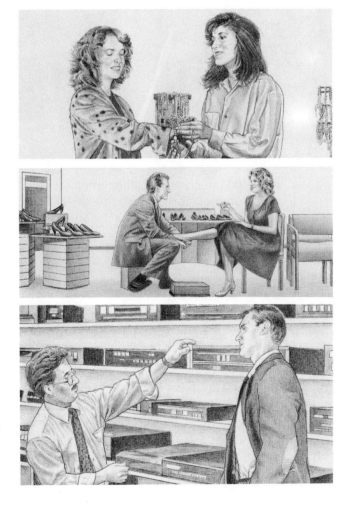

A: Good afternoon. Can I help you?

B: Yes. How much is (this/these) watch?

A: It's $175.

B: Oh. How much is (that/those) one?

A: (It's/They're) $220.

B: Oh, well. Thanks, anyway.

A: Excuse me. How much are (that/those) shoes?

B: (It's/They're) on sale for $135.

A: Well, I'll think about it. Thanks.

A: Are (this/these) stereos on sale?

B: Yes, (it/they) are.

A: And how much is (this/these) Sony?

B: (It's/They're) $350.

A: And how much are (that/these) portable stereos?

B: (It's/They're) only $99 each.

A: Oh, really? Thanks!

8 For sale!

1 Write descriptions of these four things as in the example.

bicycle for sale
Sears
2 years old
$65

I have a bicycle for sale.
It's a Sears.
It's two years old.
I'm asking $65 for it.

a) color TV for sale
   RCA
   6 months old
   $250

b) camera for sale
   Kodak
   4 years old
   $95

c) two stereo speakers for sale
   Sony
   2 years old
   $100 each

d) car for sale
   Volkswagen
   20 years old
   $1,700

2 Now write descriptions for two things you would like to sell.

9 Great gadgets! Match the ads and the pictures.

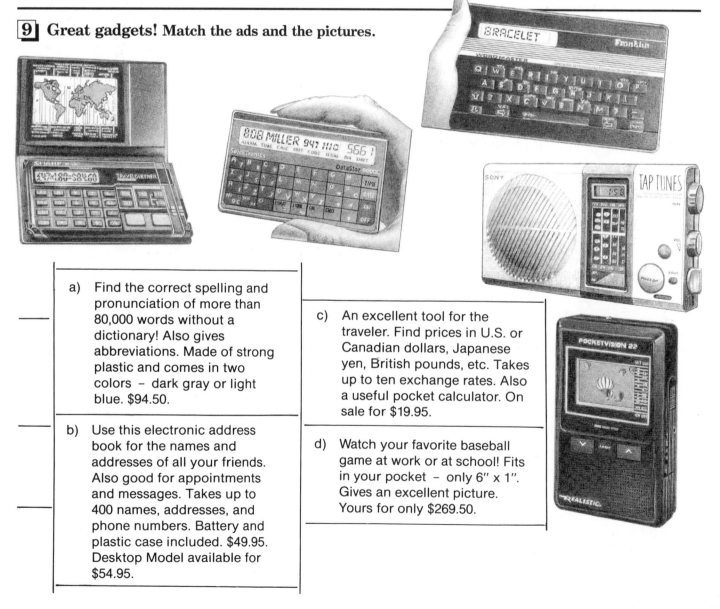

a) Find the correct spelling and pronunciation of more than 80,000 words without a dictionary! Also gives abbreviations. Made of strong plastic and comes in two colors – dark gray or light blue. $94.50.

b) Use this electronic address book for the names and addresses of all your friends. Also good for appointments and messages. Takes up to 400 names, addresses, and phone numbers. Battery and plastic case included. $49.95. Desktop Model available for $54.95.

c) An excellent tool for the traveler. Find prices in U.S. or Canadian dollars, Japanese yen, British pounds, etc. Takes up to ten exchange rates. Also a useful pocket calculator. On sale for $19.95.

d) Watch your favorite baseball game at work or at school! Fits in your pocket – only 6″ x 1″. Gives an excellent picture. Yours for only $269.50.

4 What kind of music do you like?

1 **Answer these questions. Use the phrases given and the correct pronouns.**

Do you like . . . ?   Yes, I do. I like . . . a lot.
. . . is/are OK.
No, I don't like . . . very much.

a) Do you like jazz? *Yes, I do. I like it a lot.* ....

b) Do you like horror films? *They are OK.* ....

c) Do you like Michael Jackson? ....

d) Do you like classical music? ....

e) Do you like soap operas? ....

f) Do you like Madonna? ....

g) Do you like rock music? ....

h) Do you like TV game shows? ....

2 **At the movies**

1 Find the title of each movie.

.... *A Question of $1 Million*

.... *Now and Then*

.... *The Best Man Wins*

.... *The Music Makers*

a) A crazy scientist makes a time machine and travels back in time 1,000 years. The scientist thinks life is better today. A great movie that makes you think.

b) A movie about a policewoman, a policeman, and a bank robbery. An exciting movie for people who enjoy crime movies and good photography. Lots of violence and fast action.

c) In this classic movie, John Wayne is the good guy and Humphrey Bogart is the bad guy. Both are cowboys who are in love with the same woman. Of course, the good guy marries her in the end.

2 What kinds of films are they? Write **a, b,** or **c.**

.... western   .... horror film   .... thriller   .... science fiction film

3 **Write answers to these questions.**

a) Who is your favorite actor? *My favorite actor is Eddie Murphy.*

b) Who is your favorite actress? ....

c) What is your favorite kind of music? ....

d) What is your favorite movie? ....

e) What is your favorite TV program? ....

f) Who is your favorite singer? ....

g) What is your favorite rock group? ....

h) What kind of movies do you like? ....

4 **Complete this conversation with *at, on,* or *to.***

A: Let's go .... a movie ....
Friday or Saturday.

B: OK. There's a new Tom Cruise movie
.... the Elmwood Theater.

A: Great! Let's go .... Saturday night.
What time is the movie?

B: It's .... eight and ten. Would you like
to go .... dinner before the movie?

A: Sure. There's a new Italian restaurant on Vine
Street.

B: All right. Let's meet .... the
restaurant .... Saturday ....
6 P.M.

A: OK. And then we'll go .... the eight
o'clock show.

14

5 **Choose the correct response in *B* for each sentence in *A*.**

A	*B*
a) Would you like to see a movie tonight?	.... I can't stand them.
b) Do you like soap operas?	.... I can't stand it.
c) There's a baseball game tonight.	.... She's terrific.
d) What do you think of Bette Midler?	.... How about you?
	.... That sounds good.
	.... Great! Let's go and see it.
	.... I don't agree.

6 **Write about the movies at the Film Festival.**

INTERNATIONAL FILM FESTIVAL

Century Cinema Friday, July 22	Star Theater Saturday, July 23	Varsity Theater Sunday, July 24
French movie: **A Man and a Woman** 6:00 P.M.	*Canadian movie:* **Love in Winter** 6:30 P.M.	*American movie:* **Star Wars** 5:45 P.M.
Chinese movie: **Shanghai Story** 8:00 P.M.	*Japanese movie:* **Autumn Colors** 8:15 P.M.	*Brazilian movie:* **Black Orpheus** 7:00 P.M.

a) There's a French movie at the Century Cinema on Friday, July 22, at 6:00 P.M. The movie is called *A Man and a Woman.*

b) ....

c) ....

d) ....

e) ....

f) ....

7 **Crossword puzzle: That's entertainment!**

Across clues

3   *ET* is my favorite .... fiction movie.
6   My favorite TV game .... is on Thursday at 7 o'clock.
7   I don't think Elizabeth Taylor is a very good ....
9   I like to rent .... on the weekend.
12 Tom Cruise is a great ....
13 My favorite TV .... is "Dallas."

Down clues

1   John Wayne is in a good .... on TV tonight.
2   I listen to the .... every morning on the radio.
4   I really love .... music, especially Mozart and Beethoven.
5   The movie *Psycho* is one of my favorite ....
8   Julio Iglesias is a famous Spanish ....
10 Neil Diamond is my favorite .... singer.
11 Is Whitney Houston a .... singer?

5 Tell me about your family

1 Find words in *B* to make pairs
with the words in *A*.

	A		*B*
a)	aunt	....	brother
b)	daughter	....	father
c)	mother	....	husband
d)	niece	....	nephew
e)	sister	....	son
f)	wife	....	uncle

2 Fill in the blanks below.

Singular	Plural	Singular	Plural	Singular	Plural
child	....	relative	....	woman	....
niece	....	person	....	man	....

3 Complete this conversation with questions beginning with
"What does/do . . . ?" or "Does/Do . . . ?".

A: Tell me about your family.
  What does your wife do? .... ?
B: My wife manages a hotel.

A: .... ?
B: My children are still in college.

A: .... ?
B: My daughter studies architecture.

A: .... ?
B: Yes, my sons live in a dormitory.

A: .... ?
B: My parents are both retired.

A: .... ?
B: No, my parents don't live with us. They have their own home.

A: .... ?
B: No, my wife doesn't speak English. She speaks Spanish.

4 Pronunciation: Third-person *s*

Put these words into three lists: words with /z/, /s/, and /ɪz/.

		With /z/	*With /s/*	*With /ɪz/*
asks	meets			
goes	practices			
lives	relaxes			
manages	thinks			
marries	writes			

5 Complete the answers to these questions.

a) Are the Rolling Stones a rock group?

Yes, they are.

b) Does Barbra Streisand make movies?

Yes,

c) Is Stephen King a writer?

Yes,

d) Do the Pointer Sisters sing country music?

No,

e) Are *ET* and *Star Wars* thrillers?

No,

f) Does James Bond have a family?

No,

g) Is Margaret Thatcher married?

Yes,

h) Do these questions drive you crazy?

6 Find responses in B to match sentences in A.

	A		*B*
a)	See you later.	....	No kidding!
b)	How have you been?	....	Oh, they're both OK.
c)	I have eight brothers and sisters.	....	Yeah, nice talking to you.
d)	How are your parents?	....	Things are really busy now.
e)	How's everything at work?	....	Thanks. You, too.
f)	Have a nice weekend.	....	I've been just fine, thanks.

7 **Look at these questions. Is it polite or not polite to ask them when you meet someone for the first time (in North America)?**

		Polite	*Not polite*
a)	How old is your wife?	....	....
b)	Do you work downtown?	....	....
c)	Are you religious?	....	....
d)	How much did that bag cost?	....	....
e)	Are you from Japan?	....	....
f)	What sports do you play?	....	....
g)	Why are you still single?	....	....
h)	I can't stand Democrats. How about you?	....	....

8 **Entertaining at home**

Complete the passage using the correct verbs.

bring   go   has   have   invite   leave   moves   sit   talk

American and Canadian families often .... friends and relatives over for dinner. The guests usually .... a small gift, like some flowers or a bottle of wine. Before dinner, the family and guests usually sit and .... together and .... drinks. Then everyone .... to the dining table for dinner. At the end of the meal, everyone .... dessert and coffee. After that, the family and the guests .... back to the living room and .... and talk some more. The guests usually .... around 10:00 or 10:30 P.M.

9 **Circle the word that does not belong.**

a)	brother	uncle	nephew	grandmother
b)	single	retired	married	divorced
c)	aunt	children	parents	relatives
d)	ask	talk	speak	meet
e)	help	like	love	hate

10 **Answer these questions. Use "No, . . ." and the information given.**

a) Does Sue teach Spanish?

No, she doesn't teach Spanish. She teaches French.

d) Does Lily study art?

....

....

b) Does Cathy drive a taxi?

....

....

e) Does Marie sell computers?

....

....

c) Does Chuck work in a factory?

....

....

f) Does Pierre live in the United States?

....

....

6 Do you play tennis?

1 Arrange these words in the correct order to make sentences.

a) do   on   you   what
usually   Saturday   do   ?

....

b) usually   up   don't
we   early   get

....

c) often   morning   go   in
we   the   downtown

....

d) my   gym   to   goes
the   sometimes   wife

....

e) class   always   to
Spanish   go   I   my

....

f) meet   for   always
we   lunch

....

g) we   shopping   often   the
do   the   afternoon   in

....

h) go   night   on   never
we   out   Saturday

....

2 Complete this conversation with the correct words.

A: What time do you get up .... the morning? (in/on/at)

B: I always get up .... six o'clock and run for an hour. (on/in/around) How about you?

A: Well, I usually wake up .... seven and watch TV in bed until ten. (for/from/at)

B: Oh, really? When do you go .... work? (to/in/at)

A: Twelve o'clock. I work .... the afternoon. (on/at/in)

B: What do you usually do .... your day off? (in/at/on)

A: I play basketball .... the afternoon with some friends. (in/on/at) How about you?

B: Oh, I usually go .... the gym and work out. (for/to/at)

3 **Write about Chuck's week. Use the correct form of each verb.**

MON	TUES	WED	THURS	FRI	SAT	SUN
watch the football game on TV	play tennis after work	stay home and study	do the laundry in the morning	go to the gym at 5 P.M.	invite friends over for dinner	work on the car

On Monday, Chuck watches the football game on TV. On Tuesday, he

_____

_____

_____

_____

4 **Write about yourself. Use these phrases.**

I ... every day.
 ... about once a week.
 ... about twice a month.
 ... three times a ...
 ... four times a ...
I don't ... very much.
I don't ... very often.
I never ...

CLEANING UP YOUR ROOM ONCE A YEAR... JUST ISN'T ENOUGH!

a) (write letters) *I write letters about once a month.*

b) (eat out) _____

c) (play sports) _____

d) (see a movie) _____

e) (watch TV) _____

f) (clean my room) _____

g) (listen to the radio) _____

h) (cook for myself) _____

i) (go shopping) _____

5 **Which verbs go with which nouns? Write the nouns under the correct verbs.**

do   go   listen to   play   watch

aerobics	housework	the radio	sports
a ballgame	the laundry	roller skating	a talk show
hiking	music	shopping	tennis
homework	a play	skiing	TV

6 **Read these ads. Where can you do the following?**

		Hiking Club	*YWCA/YMCA*	*Adult Education Program*
a)	play indoor sports	....	....	....
b)	do outdoor activities	....	....	....
c)	take evening courses	....	....	....
d)	go dancing	....	....	....
e)	learn a hobby	....	....	....
f)	enjoy nature	....	....	....

Do you enjoy the outdoors? Do you like camping and meeting people? Do you need exercise? Join the Hiking Club! We go on a different hike every week. Sometimes we go on a two-day hike. Call 745-1191.

Join the YWCA or YMCA! Look at our new activities! Aerobics, squash, handball, racquetball. For anyone from 9 to 90! Singles and families welcome. Friday night teen disco, Saturday night oldies night! Phone us at 235-7439.

ADULT EDUCATION PROGRAM at Monroe High School. Mon.–Fri. 6:00–9:00 P.M. Fall classes: photography, computers for business, typing and word processing, Chinese cooking, and Spanish, French, and Italian language classes. For more information, call 535-6845.

23

7 **Check the correct responses to complete the conversation.**

A: Do you get much exercise?

B: .... How often?

.... Yes, I do.

.... How about you?

A: How often do you exercise?

B: .... I watch TV a lot.

.... Yes, I often do.

.... About three times a week.

A: What do you usually do?

B: .... I usually go swimming and play racquetball.

.... No, I never do.

.... I go straight home after work.

A: Where do you go swimming?

B: .... Every day from 5 to 6.

.... I always go to the YWCA.

.... No, I play tennis.

A: You're really in good shape!

B: .... Yeah, I'm a real couch potato.

.... Oh, are you?

.... Thanks a lot.

8 **Crossword puzzle: Routines**

Across clues

2 Do you .... at the pool or the beach?
3 I .... the train to work in the morning around seven.
4 What time do you .... up in the morning?
5 Do you .... to work or take the bus?
6 I .... out at the gym on Saturday.
7 I .... work around 5 P.M. every day.
9 I .... an hour a day walking.
11 Do you always .... the bus to school?
12 What newspaper do you .... ?

Down clues

1 Do you .... TV very much?
2 School usually .... at nine o'clock.
3 They always .... their house on Saturdays.
5 After I run, I .... a lot of water.
8 I always .... pretty late on Sundays.
10 What sports do you .... ?

7 It was terrific!

1 Spelling check

> *Past Tense – Regular Verbs*
>
> Add **-ed** (most verbs):   want – want**ed**
> Add **-d** (verbs ending in **e**):   live – liv**ed**
> Add **-ied** (verbs ending
>   consonant + **y**):   study – stud**ied**

Spell the past tense of these verbs.

a) add ....

b) carry ....

c) dance ....

d) enjoy ....

e) like ....

f) listen ....

g) marry ....

h) phone ....

i) stay ....

j) try ....

k) visit ....

l) work ....

2 Complete this postcard, using the past tense of the verbs.

Dear Karen,

Hi, there! My vacation .... (be) great! I .... (visit) my friends in Puerto Rico. I .... (stay) at a nice hotel near a beautiful beach. We .... (rent) a car and .... (travel) around the island.

I .... (try) to learn windsurfing, but it .... (be) difficult. I .... (enjoy) the food and really .... (like) the fresh fruit. I .... (talk) to a lot of local people there. I'm really glad I .... (study) Spanish in high school. See you soon!

                    Love,

                    Ken

3 **Complete the missing verbs with past tense forms of *be* and *do*. Then number these sentences from 1 to 12 to make a conversation.**

A

[ ] Oh, good! And what .... you do in Spain?

[/] How *was* .... your trip to Europe?

[ ] Where .... you go?

[ ] .... you see a bullfight in Spain?

[ ] Oh, really? I enjoy them. And .... you go to Portugal?

[ ] So how long .... you in Spain?

B

[ ] We went to Spain. It .... great.

[ ] No, we .... I don't like bullfights.

[ ] We .... there for two weeks.

[ ] No, we .... We .... have time, unfortunately.

[ ] The trip .... pretty good, but the weather .... a bit cool.

[ ] Oh, we .... the usual sightseeing and shopping.

---

4 **Write questions for these responses.**

A: How ....?
B: Oh, my weekend was terrific, thanks.

A: What ....?
B: Well, on Saturday, I ran in the marathon. Guess what! I was third!

A: Congratulations! And what ....
....?
B: I didn't do much on Sunday until the evening. Then I went to see the new James Bond movie.

A: Did ....?
B: Yes, I really enjoyed it. It's worth seeing. Well, how about you?

   How ....?
A: Oh, it was terrible.

B: Really? What ....?

A: Nothing much. That was the trouble!

5 A California vacation

Number these sentences from a letter from 1 to 7.

.... We rode the cable cars, saw Chinatown and Fisherman's Wharf, and took a cruise around San Francisco Bay.

.... Then we rented a car and drove to Palm Springs. It's about three hours from Los Angeles. We played golf there and took a tour.

.... Well, that's about all for now. I'll tell you about the rest of my trip when I get back.

1 We had a great vacation in California!

.... After San Francisco, we went to Los Angeles. We loved Hollywood and Universal Studios, but I didn't care much for the city itself.

.... From Palm Springs, we went to San Diego. It's a beautiful city, and the zoo is really interesting.

.... We started our trip in San Francisco.

6 Use the cues to answer these questions with the past tense and the correct pronouns.

a) Where did you buy that bag? (in Mexico)

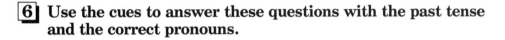
I bought it in Mexico.

b) Where did you meet your husband? (in Japan)

....

c) When did you see the movie? (on Thursday night)

....

d) Where did you get those sunglasses? (at Macy's)

....

e) When did you do your homework? (this afternoon)

....

f) Where did you learn French? (in high school)

....

g) When did you visit Bill and Mary? (last summer)

....

h) Where did you hear about the concert? (on the news)

....

i) Where did you take your mother for her birthday? (to an Italian restaurant)

....

j) What did you buy me for my birthday? (something special)

....

7 **How many connections can you make between these words and the categories?**

Food

On vacation

buy	read
climb	run
cook	study
drink	tour
eat	travel
fly	visit
jog	walk
learn	write
make	

Sports and exercise

School

8 **Read this newspaper story. Then read the statements the police took from two suspects, Tony and Rita Buckby. How many differences can you find between Tony's and Rita's statements?**

Thieves Steal Vanderfill Jewels!

A man and a woman entered the home of millionaire Dorothy Vanderfill in New Jersey at 9 P.M. last Saturday and stole a $60,000 diamond necklace and some jewels.

Tony's statement

We left our house at 8 P.M. and drove downtown for dinner. We had dinner at Buddy's Steak House. After dinner, we went for a walk and did some shopping. I bought some magazines, and Rita bought some candy. Then we went for a drive along the lake. We got home at 11 P.M. and went to bed.

Rita's statement

We left our house at 8 P.M. and drove downtown for dinner. We parked in front of Buddy's Steak House and had dinner. After dinner, we drove around Chinatown and looked at the shops. We came home at 10:30 P.M. and watched TV until midnight.

8 You can't miss it!

1 **Use the map to answer the questions. Use these prepositions:**

across from   near   next to   on   on the corner of   opposite

a) Where's the nearest bank?

There's one on 1st Street.

b) Is there a post office near here?

....

....

c) I'm looking for a drugstore.

....

....

d) Where's the Star Hotel?

....

....

e) Is there a library around here?

....

....

```
                    KENT
         ┌──────────────┐        ┌──────────────────────┐
         │  ┌─────────┐ │        │  ┌─→ Star Hotel       │
         │  │←supermarket│        │  │                    │
         │  ├─────────┤ │        │  └                    │
         │  │ bank    │ │        │                        │
         └──┴─────────┴─┘        └──────────────────────┘
                    BROWN
         ┌──────────────┐        ┌──────────────────────┐
         │     drugstore│        │ gas station          │
    1st  │   library │↓ │  2nd   │ │↓  department   3rd  │
         │         ↓    │        │ │   store             │
         │              │        │ └──  movie           │
         │              │        │       theater        │
         └──────────────┘        └──────────────────────┘
                    ASH
         ┌──────────────┐        ┌──────────────────────┐
         │   ┌────┐      │        │          post →      │
         │   │YWCA│ ↑    │        │          office      │
         │   └────┘      │        │                      │
         │  laundromat│  │        │                      │
         └──────────────┘        └──────────────────────┘
                    LIME
```

2 **Find responses in B to match sentences in A.**

	A		B
a)	What's your new house like?	....	Yes, I like it a lot.
		....	It's really nice.
		....	Yes, it is.
b)	How big is it?	....	It has five rooms.
		....	Yes, it's very big.
		....	No, it's not very big.
c)	What's the neighborhood like?	....	They are very friendly.
		....	Yes, I like them.
		....	It's very quiet.
d)	Is there a bus stop nearby?	....	Yes, there are.
		....	Yes, just across the street.
		....	Yes, it is.
e)	Gee, it sounds like a nice place.	....	Yes, that's terrific.
		....	No kidding.
		....	Thanks. I really like it.

29

3 **Look at these two street maps. There are ten differences between them. Find the other eight. Write about them as in the examples below.**

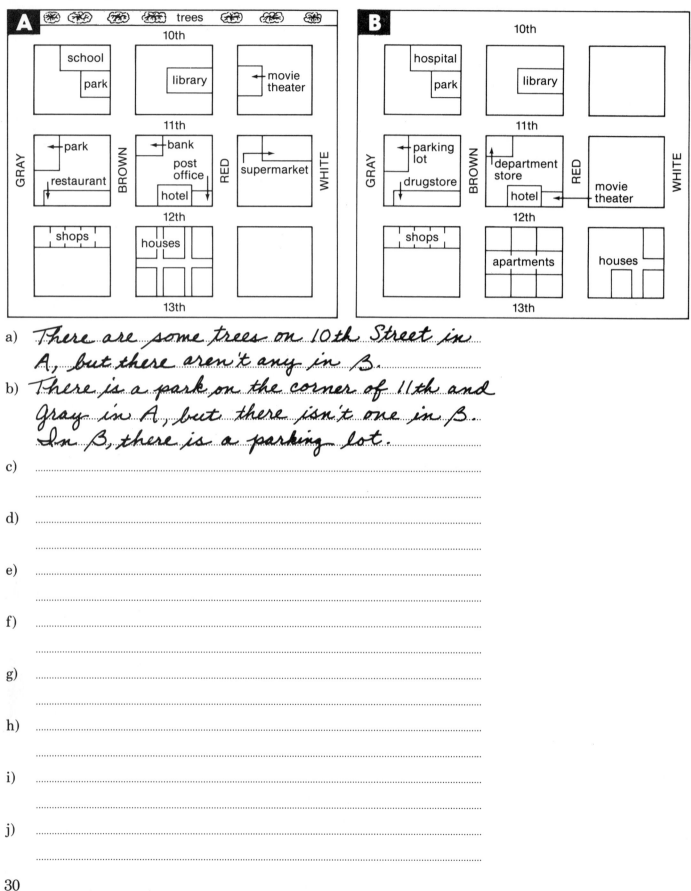

a) *There are some trees on 10th Street in A, but there aren't any in B.*

b) *There is a park on the corner of 11th and Gray in A, but there isn't one in B. In B, there is a parking lot.*

c) ....

....

d) ....

....

e) ....

....

f) ....

....

g) ....

....

h) ....

....

i) ....

....

j) ....

....

4 **Underline one wrong thing in each ad.**

a) For rent: Large house in quiet location. Near schools and public transportation. Good for family with children. Right next to the airport and freeway. Call Mr. Hill at 932-5570.

b) Small studio apartment available. 4 bedrooms. New carpet, bed, and stove. $350. Phone 442-8541.

c) Unfurnished house in quiet neighborhood. Available Nov. 1. Near schools and shops. New carpets, sofa, beds, and refrigerator. Call John at 437-9982.

d) Room (200 square feet) available in comfortable home. Completely furnished with bed, TV, and carpet. No kitchen. Near the university. Good for family with children. Phone Mrs. Melrose mornings 389-4357.

e) Beautiful new house on Elm St. Only $500 a month. 3 bedrooms, double garage, garden. House only 30 years old but in good condition. Riley Realtors.

f) Mobile home for rent. Very cheap. 1,200 square feet. 2 bedrooms, bath, and kitchen. $1,800/week. Furnished. Call 852-6103 now.

5 **Answer these questions about your city or neighborhood like this:**

Yes, there is. There's one on James Street.
No, there isn't.
Yes, there are. There are some on James and Fourth.
No, there aren't.

a) Are there any good restaurants around here?

....

b) Is there a drive-in movie theater in this city?

....

c) Is there a pay phone nearby?

....

d) Are there any good clothing shops near here?

....

e) Is there a museum in this city?

....

f) Is there a police station near this school?

....

g) Are there any good bookstores in town?

....

6 Crossword puzzle: Places

Across clues

3 I need to wash my hands. Is there a .... around here?

5 Do you have any coins? I want to use a pay ....

6 Is there a bus stop on this .... ?

7 What's that big .... across the street?

10 What .... do your kids go to?

12 Is this a nice .... to live in?

14 I need some stamps. Is there a .... office around here?

15 I don't have any money. I need to go to the ....

17 There's a good Mexican .... near here.

19 I need to get some medicine at the ....

20 The Westin .... is a nice place to stay.

21 I need to buy some eggs. Where's the nearest .... store?

Down clues

1 I need to buy a dictionary. Is there a good .... around here?

2 There are fifty stores in the .... center.

4 I need gas. Where's the nearest gas .... ?

8 I always wash my clothes on Saturday at the ....

9 Do you exercise every day at the .... ?

10 What .... do you go to for your groceries?

11 Let's go to the coffee .... for a snack and something to drink.

13 I just borrowed this book from the ....

16 Do you like art? There's a nice art .... near here.

18 I love movies. Is there a good movie .... around here?

9 Which one is Judy?

1 Look at these clothes and accessories. How many words can you list in each category?

Women only	Both men and women		Men only
belt	bracelet	gloves	shirt
bikini	cap	jeans	three-piece suit
blouse	cufflinks	miniskirt	tie
boxer shorts	dress	pants	T-shirt
bra	earrings	scarf	

2 Spelling check: Verb + -ing

Add **-ing** (most verbs):	walk – walk**ing**
Drop **e** and add **-ing**:	give – giv**ing**
Double the final consonant and add **-ing**:	sit – sit**ting**

Write the **-ing** form of these verbs.

come ....   have ....   run ....   swim ....

do ....   help ....   sell ....   take ....

get ....   love ....   smoke ....   work ....

3 Find the opposites.

a)	big	e)	good	......	bad	......	noisy
b)	old	f)	quiet	......	boring	......	small
c)	cheap	g)	straight	......	curly	......	tall
d)	short	h)	exciting	......	expensive	......	young

4 **Complete these descriptions. Use the present continuous and the verbs below. Remember to use the correct form of the verb *be*.**

a) collect   listen   sell   wait   work   jog   ride   talk   walk

A woman *is walking* .... her dog. Two policemen ....

.... to a driver. A boy .... newspapers. A girl

.... a skateboard. Some construction workers ....

.... on a building. Some people .... at the bus stop.

Two women .... They .... to

music. A mail carrier .... the mail.

b) dance   play   sit   stand   eat   serve   smoke   talk

Dan and Cindy .... Keiko ....

drinks. Angela .... on the sofa. She ....

.... to Kim. Marie and Joe .... cards. Helmut

.... a pizza. Carlos .... by the

window. He .... a pipe.

34

5 Circle two things in each description that do not match the picture. Then write the correct information.

a   b   c   d

a)   He's in his thirties. He's pretty tall. He has straight black hair. He's wearing jeans and a T-shirt.

b)   She's about 50. She's pretty tall. She has long hair. She's wearing jeans and boots. She's standing next to a motorcycle.

c)   She has short brown hair and she's wearing glasses. She's fairly short, and she's about 25. She's wearing a blouse and a skirt.

d)   He's about 10. He has curly blond hair. He's wearing shorts and a black and white shirt. He's carrying some magazines.

6 Complete this conversation with questions in the present continuous.

A: What time *are you going to the party* ?
B: I'm going to the party at 8.

A: How _____ ?
B: I'm going there by taxi.

A: Who _____ with?
B: I'm going with Joe.

A: What _____ ?
B: I'm wearing a sweater and jeans.

A: How long _____ ?
B: I'm staying till about 10.

A: Where _____ ?
B: I'm going to a disco after the party. Do you want to come?

A: Sure!

7 **Write descriptions of Pierre du Pont and Diane Jones on a separate paper.**

Mr. Grant   Pierre du Pont   Diane Jones

Mr. Grant is in his fifties. He is fairly short. He has dark hair and a moustache. He is wearing a suit, and he is carrying a briefcase.

8 **Culture quiz**

Read this information about what people do in North America. Is it the same in your country? Check "Same" or "Different."

		Same	Different
a)	Children don't wear uniforms to public schools.	....	....
b)	Many adults like to wear shorts in the summer.	....	....
c)	People often wear casual clothes, like jeans, to the theater or to concerts.	....	....
d)	Some men like to grow a moustache or beard.	....	....
e)	Some women like to wear nail polish.	....	....
f)	Both men and women sometimes dye their hair.	....	....
g)	People are not smoking so much these days.	....	....
h)	Many restaurants have nonsmoking sections.	....	....
i)	Male and female college students sometimes live in the same dormitory.	....	....
j)	Many young people don't live at home with their parents after they get jobs.	....	....
k)	Parents don't usually choose dates for their sons and daughters.	....	....
l)	People usually serve wine, beer, and soft drinks at parties.	....	....

10 Guess what happened!

1 **Complete the verb table.**

Present	Past	Past participle	Present	Past	Past participle
be	was	been	go	....	gone
break	....	broken	....	knew	....
drive	drove	....	see	....	....
forget	....	....	....	....	taken

2 **Have you ever done any of these things? Check (✓) the ones that you have done.**

.... a) collected money for charity

.... b) been in a traffic accident

.... c) eaten oysters

.... d) gone skiing

.... e) been to a rock concert

.... f) gone to a circus

.... g) seen the movie *Batman*

.... h) gone rock climbing

.... i) been sailing

.... j) stayed in a hotel

Now write sentences using these phrases.

I have often . . .
I have . . . several times.
I have never . . .

a) *I have collected money for charity several times.*

b) ....

c) ....

d) ....

e) ....

f) ....

g) ....

h) ....

i) ....

j) ....

3 **Read these newspaper stories and complete each story with the verbs given.**

a) had   lifted   ran   rented   said   saw   spent   swam   was

A group of tourists on a tour of the Grand Canyon .... a free
helicopter ride on a recent vacation. The group .... a boat for a
ride through the canyon, but the boat .... into a rock and sank.
The tourists .... to the shore and .... the night in a
cave. The next morning, a rescue team in a helicopter .... them
and .... them out of the canyon. "It .... the best part
of our tour," .... one of the tourists.

b) arrived   discovered   got   heard   stopped   took   took

A passenger traveling to California nearly .... in New Zealand
on Sunday. The passenger .... a flight from Chicago. He
.... an announcement and .... on the plane. Two
hours later, he .... it was a flight to Auckland, New Zealand,
and not Oakland, California. When the plane .... in
Honolulu, he .... another flight back to California.

4 **Choose the correct response.**

a) I lost my wallet on Friday.

.... That's terrific!

.... That's terrible!

.... That's great!

b) I forgot my husband's birthday
yesterday.

.... Oh, sorry.

.... How embarrassing!

.... Good for you!

c) My parents gave me a new car
for my birthday.

.... Lucky you!

.... Have you?

.... How awful!

d) Wendy and Tim just got
married.

.... Don't worry!

.... Sounds great!

.... Oh, that's terrific!

5 **What happened to Bill? Read this description and number the events from 1 to 12 in the order in which they occurred.**

.... The guy there drove me back to my car and fixed the tire.

.... Then, luckily, someone stopped and helped me. He was a mechanic, and he fixed the engine.

..1.. I had a terrible experience on Saturday.

.... So then I walked for about two miles to a gas station.

..12.. What a day! Next time, I'll take the bus!

.... I tried to get the engine to start, but nothing happened.

.... I got a flat tire on the freeway.

.... But half an hour later, the car broke down.

.... I looked in the trunk for the spare tire, but it was flat, too.

.... Next, I stood by my car for thirty minutes, but no one stopped.

.... Then I got in the car again and drove off.

.... This time, it was the engine.

6 **Write questions using "Have you ever . . . ?" based on the statements below.**

a) *Have you ever been to Disneyland?*
I went to Disneyland last month.

b) ....
I was in a car accident yesterday.

c) ....
I flew in a helicopter last summer.

d) ....
I went to Europe last year.

e) ....
I saw a Chinese opera on Friday night.

f) ....
I tried windsurfing last weekend.

7 Which nouns go with which verbs? Write the nouns under the correct verbs.

drive	have	ride	take

an accident   a flight   a trip
a bicycle   a horse   a truck
a bus   a motorcycle   a vacation
a car   a taxi   a van
a flat tire   a train

8 Crossword puzzle: Present perfect

Across clues

4 Have you ever .... cross-country skiing?
5 Do you know the teacher's phone number? I have .... it.
8 I haven't .... my bike yet. It's only $150. Do you want to buy it?
9 Have you ever .... a letter to a newspaper?
11 Tom's new sports car is great! Have you ever .... one?
14 Have you ever .... German?
15 Steve Martin's new movie is really funny. Have you ever .... one of his films?

Down clues

1 Have you ever .... a movie star?
2 Have you ever .... something at a swap meet?
3 I loved Vancouver! Have you ever .... to Canada?
4 I took the wrong exit off the freeway. It was terrible! Have you ever .... lost on one?
5 Have you ever .... on Singapore Airlines?
6 I went horseback riding last week. Have you ever .... a horse?
7 Have you ever .... surfing?
10 Have you ever .... a cruise?
12 I've never .... Thai food, but I hear it's delicious.
13 Have you ever .... your luggage on a flight?

11 It's an interesting place

1 Put the words in B's answers in the correct order.

A: Is your hometown a nice place?
B: beautiful and yes it's beach an has excellent it

....

A: What's the weather like?
B: the very it's summer nice in

....

A: And how about the winter?
B: lot it's a very snows cold it in winter and the

....

A: Is it an interesting town?
B: with an yes museum interesting it's good a place

....

A: Is it expensive there?
B: not and no too cheap rents expensive it's are

....

2 Choose the correct word to complete each statement.

a) Prices are very high in New York City.

Everything is pretty .... there.
(cheap, expensive, huge)

b) My hometown is not an exciting place.

The nightlife there is really ....
(fascinating, interesting, boring)

c) Rome is a beautiful old city.

There are not many .... buildings.
(big, modern, small)

d) Some parts of this city are fairly dangerous.

They are not very .... late at night.
(safe, noisy, quiet)

e) Athens is a quiet city in the winter.

The streets are never .... at that time of the year.
(crowded, clean, safe)

3 **Read about these cities and underline two pieces of information in each description that don't agree.**

Tokyo is Japan's most exciting city. It is a city where old Japan meets modern Japan, with beautiful new skyscrapers and fascinating old temples. It is a very busy city. The streets are always empty, and the subways are crowded. It is also one of the most expensive cities in the world. A room in a good hotel only costs a few dollars.

Los Angeles is the biggest city in California. It is famous for its freeways, its movie stars, and its smog. It has excellent museums, universities, and shopping centers. Los Angeles is not far from Disneyland, which is only 1,500 miles away. Visitors like to go to the film studios and to drive along Hollywood Boulevard. Los Angeles has a warm climate, clean air, and good beaches nearby.

4 **On vacation**

Make suggestions with "You should . . ." or "You shouldn't . . ." using the sentences below.

a) Take a bus tour of the city.

You should take a bus tour of the city.

b) Don't stay near the airport.

You shouldn't stay near the airport.

c) Go in the spring or the summer.

....

d) Don't miss the National Museum.

....

e) See the new zoo.

....

f) Don't walk alone late at night.

....

g) Change your money at a bank.

....

h) Don't change money on the street.

....

i) Don't drink the tap water.

....

---

5 **Use *and* or *but* to join these sentences.**

> Use **and** for additional information: It is a beautiful city, **and** it has a good climate.
>
> Use **but** for contrasting information: It is a very old city, **but** it has a modern subway system.

a) Paris is a very interesting place. It has beautiful architecture.

Paris is a very interesting place, and it has beautiful architecture.

b) London is an exciting city. It has great nightclubs.

....

....

c) My hometown is a beautiful place. The climate there is too cold for me in the winter.

....

....

d) Australia is a beautiful country. It has a very good climate.

....

....

e) Tokyo is an exciting place for a vacation. It is very good for shopping.

....

....

f) Washington, D.C., does not have a very good climate. It is a very interesting place to visit.

....

....

---

6 **Circle the word that does not belong.**

a) old   small   modern   new

b) fascinating   interesting   wonderful   horrible

c) nice   noisy   dirty   dangerous

d) hot   warm   ugly   cold

e) excellent   small   big   huge

7 **Check if these sentences need *a* or *an*. Then add *a* or *an* where necessary.**

> Use **a** or **an** with adjective + singular noun: It is **an old city.**
> It has **a new park.**
>
> Use no article with **be** + adjective: It **is old.**

a) .... Restaurants are very cheap in Mexico.

b) ✓........ Copenhagen is ^*a*^ clean city.

c) .... Sydney Harbour is beautiful.

d) .... Dallas has big airport.

e) .... Apartments are expensive in
Washington, D.C.

f) .... London is crowded city in the summer.

g) .... Toronto has good museums.

h) .... Rio is exciting place to visit.

8 **Complete this description of London with *is* or *has*.**

London .... Britain's biggest city. It .... a very old city and dates back to the Romans.

It .... a city of beautiful buildings and churches, and it .... many beautiful parks. It

also .... some of the best museums in the world. London .... very crowded in summer.

It .... a popular city with foreign tourists and .... more than eight million visitors a year.

The city .... famous for its shopping and .... many excellent department stores.

London .... an excellent underground railway system, so it .... easy for tourists to get

around. There are plenty of good restaurants in London. You can get excellent British food, and

London .... lots of good Indian, Chinese, Japanese, French, Italian, and Greek restaurants.

12 It really works!

1 Match the words and definitions.

a) drugstore
b) fever
c) hangover
d) indigestion
e) juice
f) medicine
g) ointment
h) shampoo
i) insomnia

.... a pain in your stomach after eating

.... an uncomfortable feeling after drinking too much alcohol

.... something you take to cure an illness

.... a place where you buy medicine

.... a hot feeling when you have a cold or the flu

.... difficulty going to sleep

.... a cream used mainly for burns and other skin problems

.... a liquid soap for washing your hair

.... a drink made from a fruit or vegetable

2 Rewrite the requests below using *can, could, may,* or *would.*

Can I have . . . , please? May I have . . . , please?
Could I have . . . , please? I would like . . . , please.

a) Give me something for a headache.

May I have something for a headache, please?

b) Give me some vitamin tablets.

....

c) I need some throat medicine.

....

d) I want a box of tissues.

....

e) Give me a large tube of toothpaste.

....

f) I want a small jar of honey.

....

g) Give me a bottle of orange juice.

....

h) I need something for the flu.

....

45

3 **Draw a line from each phrase to words in the list. How many connections can you make for each phrase?**

a bottle of

a box of

a can of

a carton of

butter
cookies
jam
juice
matches
milk
7-Up
shaving cream
sunburn lotion
tablets
tissues
toothpaste

a jar of

a package of

a tube of

4 **Use *should* and the phrases below to give advice for each problem.**

.... drink hot chicken soup

.... take aspirin

.... use some lotion

.... take some cough drops

..*a*.. go to bed and rest

.... drink water with baking soda

.... drink warm milk

a) a backache *For a backache, you should go to bed and rest.*

b) a headache ....

c) a cold ....

d) indigestion ....

e) a sore throat ....

f) insomnia ....

g) a sunburn ....

46

5 **Read this passage. Then circle *T* (true) or *F* (false) for the statements below.**

Getting to Sleep

Normally, people sleep between seven and eight hours a day, although some people need less than this and some may need more. But millions of people have trouble getting to sleep every night.

According to sleep expert Dr. Robert Schachter, many people do not know why they have difficulty sleeping. Most people know that tea and coffee often make it difficult to go to sleep because they contain caffeine. But some medicines, such as cold tablets, also contain caffeine and interfere with sleep. Sleeping pills may help you fall asleep, but when you wake the next morning you don't feel refreshed.

Our living habits also affect our sleep. Busy people who are under stress during the day may not be able to calm down and fall asleep at night. Eating just before going to bed may also keep you awake.

Dr. Schachter says that you will sleep more easily if your bedroom is used only for sleep. You shouldn't use your bedroom as a conference room, a TV room, or an exercise room. You should also establish a regular sleeping schedule, but don't go to bed until you are tired. Try to go to bed at the same time every night and get up at the same time every morning. And if all this does not work, try counting sheep!

a) T   F   Everyone needs eight hours sleep a night.

b) T   F   Caffeine helps you fall asleep.

c) T   F   Active people might have trouble falling asleep easily.

d) T   F   You should be careful about eating just before you go to bed.

e) T   F   It is a good idea to have a TV near your bed.

f) T   F   You should have regular sleeping hours.

6 **Choose the correct prepositions to complete the conversation.**

A: I need something .... insomnia.
(for/on/with)

B: Try these tablets. Take two .... the evening. (at/in/on)   And don't drink a lot .... coffee. (at/for/of)

A: OK. Thank you.

B: And sometimes warm milk helps you go .... sleep. (for/in/to)

A: Really? I'll try it.

B: Anything else?

A: Yes, can I have a bottle .... Valium tablets, please? (of/to/with)

B: Oh, you should get a prescription .... the doctor for those. (for/from/to)

7 **Crossword puzzle: Oh, doctor!**

Across clues

3   I burned my .... cooking dinner.
5   I broke my .... and had to go to the dentist.
6   Brian always talks too much. He has a big ....
8   I ate too much last night. Now I have a ....
13 My .... hurts when I breathe.
15 I picked up three heavy bags yesterday, and now I have a ....
17 I hurt my .... when I lifted the box of books.
18 Your .... look nice. Are you wearing contact lenses?
19 Have you been to the beach? Your face is sunburned and your .... is red.

Down clues

1   Carol has a beautiful necklace around her ....
2   I have a sore .... It hurts when I swallow.
3   Tim has really big .... He always wears boots.
4   The teacher has the .... She can't come to school today.
7   I need to see the dentist. I have a bad ....
9   I worked out at the gym. Now my .... are really sore.
10 She usually wears two rings on her left ....
11 My head feels terrible. I have a very bad ....
12 I need some ear drops. I have a pain in my ....
14 My .... feels cold. I'll put on my hat.
16 Sharon runs very fast. She has strong ....

13 May I take your order, please?

1 **Use one or more words to complete this conversation between a waiter and a customer.**

A: May I .... your order, please?

B: Yes, ... a steak, please. I'd like it well done.

A: And .... you like a salad?

B: Yes, ...

A: What .... dressing would you like?

B: French, please.

A: Would .... drink?

B: Yes, ... coffee,

    ....

A: Anything else?

B: No, that'll be .... , thanks.

2 **Arrange these menu items into the categories below.**

baked fish	chocolate cake	ice cream	small salad
beans	clam chowder	lemon meringue pie	soda
beer	coffee	lobster	spaghetti and meatballs
broccoli	french fries	onion soup	steak
carrot cake	fresh peas	oysters	sweet corn
carrots	fried chicken	roast beef	tea
cheesecake	garlic bread	shrimp cocktail	wine

Side orders   *Appetizers*   *Entrees*

Desserts   *Vegetables*   *Drinks*

3 **Read this description of what usually happens when you eat at a restaurant. Number the sentences from 1 to 11 in the order each event usually happens.**

.... The cook prepares your meal.

.... The waiter or waitress brings you a menu.

.... The waiter or waitress brings your check, and then you pay the bill and leave.

...*1*... The host or hostess greets you.

.... The waiter or waitress then brings your meal.

.... You look through the menu and decide what you want to eat and drink.

.... Then he or she takes the order to the kitchen.

.... When you are ready to leave, you ask for the check.

.... The waiter or waitress writes down your order.

.... Someone takes you to a table, and you sit down.

.... You eat your meal and then have dessert if you want.

"*Here comes yours now, I think.*"

Drawing by O'Brian; © 1964 The New Yorker Magazine, Inc.

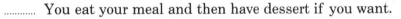

4 **Gina wants a pizza delivered to her home. Complete this telephone conversation.**

A: Hello. Domino Pizza. May ....?

B: I'd like to order a pizza, please.

A: Sure. Would ....?

B: No, not a large one. I'd like a small one.

A: What kind of ....?

B: For a topping, I'll have cheese, olives, and sausage.

A: Fine. And would ....?

B: Yes, I'll have a large Coke, please.

A: Could ....?

B: My name's Gina Lanzo. And my phone number is 821-3003.

A: And may ....?

B: My address is 2389 Oak Street.

A: OK. We'll bring your pizza in twenty minutes.

B: Thanks. Bye.

5 Choose the correct response.

a) Anything else?

.... Not right now, thanks.

.... You're welcome.

.... Not at all.

b) Thank you so much for the meal.

.... You're welcome.

.... What will you have?

.... No, that'll be all, thanks.

c) Goodbye now. Take care.

.... I'm glad you liked it.

.... Thanks. You, too.

.... Yes, please.

d) Good night. See you soon.

.... Not at all.

.... I hope so. Bye.

.... No, thank you.

6 Choose the correct word to complete these sentences.

a) In restaurants, customers usually leave .... for the waiter or waitress. (checks, orders, tips)

b) People who work in restaurants usually get fairly low .... (bills, fares, salaries)

c) In a restaurant, the waiter or waitress takes your .... (menu, order, service)

d) Chocolate is a popular ice cream .... (drink, flavor, meal)

e) At many restaurants, you need to make .... to get a table. (information, an invitation, a reservation)

f) Many people like .... on their salad. (dessert, dressing, soup)

g) In Canada and the United States, the check in a restaurant does not usually .... a service charge. (cost, include, spend)

h) Yogurt is a healthy milk .... (flavor, order, product)

7 **Read these ads and then answer the questions.**

DYNASTY RESTAURANT

2nd floor, Ward Shopping Center
Open 11 A.M. to 10:00 P.M.
7 days a week
** Excellent Chinese cuisine **

Shrimp with lobster sauce
Spicy fried beef or chicken
Lemon chicken

Vegetarian orders also available

Dine in or take out!
For free delivery call 922-4860

Cafe Athens

Delicious coffee and espresso
Beer, wine, and drinks
in the Greek Bar
Light snacks and meals

Live music every night!

Belly dancing at 10 P.M.
Friday & Saturday only
$5 cover charge

Located opposite Sam's Bowling
Monday–Saturday
7 P.M. till 2 A.M.
No personal checks
or credit cards

Come to the YumYum Restaurant!

Breakfast, lunch, dinner
Open 24 hours
Family restaurant
Our specialties – desserts:
fresh baked pies & cakes daily

Meals start at $4.00

VISA and MasterCard welcome
Sorry, no delivery

1st & High St.   677-1257

—— Giorgio's —— Italian Restaurant

310 S. Pine Ave.
647-9928 for reservations

Lunch & Dinner Service
Monday–Saturday
11:30 A.M.–11:30 P.M.

Spaghetti, lasagna, pizza
the best in town!
Outdoor seating available
in our new patio
Reservations necessary

Most major credit
cards accepted
All meals cooked to order
by our famous chef, Giorgio

a)   Which restaurant is open at 3 A.M.? ....

b)   Which restaurant has Italian food? ....

c)   Which restaurant serves breakfast? ....

d)   Which restaurant has entertainment? ....

e)   Which restaurants are open on Sunday? ....

f)   Which restaurant delivers meals to your home? ....

g)   Which restaurants accept credit cards? ....

14 It's the greatest!

1 Match each word with a definition.

a) avenue

b) beach

c) desert

d) forest

e) island

f) lake

g) mountain

h) ocean

i) valley

j) volcano

.... a dry, sandy place where it doesn't rain much and there aren't many plants

.... a large area of land covered with trees

.... the area where the ocean meets the land, usually with sand or rocks

.... an area of water with land all around it

.... the area of land between two rows of hills or mountains, often with a river running through it

.... a mountain with a hole at the top, which sometimes gives off hot gas and lava

.... a very high hill with trees or covered with snow at the top

.... a wide street in a city, or a road between two rows of trees

.... an area of salt water that covers a large part of the earth

.... a piece of land with water all around it

2 Spelling check: Comparatives

Add **-er:**	cheap – cheap**er**
Add **-r:**	nice – nic**er**
Drop **y** and add **-ier:**	dirty – dirt**ier**
Double the final consonant and add **-er:**	hot – hot**ter**

Give the comparative form of these adjectives.

a) big ....

b) busy ....

c) cool ....

d) dry ....

e) friendly ....

f) high ....

g) large ....

h) long ....

i) noisy ....

j) safe ....

k) warm ....

l) wet ....

3 **Write questions using the cues below and the comparative forms of the adjectives.**

a)   Which is *Colder* .... (cold), Ottawa or Vancouver?

b)   Which is *more modern* .... (modern), Brasília or Rio?

c)   Which is .... (big), France or Spain?

d)   Which is .... (cheap), Tokyo or Los Angeles?

e)   Which is .... (exciting), Madrid or Lisbon?

f)   Which is .... (dangerous), mountain climbing or windsurfing?

g)   Which is .... (interesting), Hong Kong or Taipei?

h)   Which is .... (old), Budapest or Warsaw?

i)   Which is .... (hot) in summer, Egypt or Jordan?

4 **Use the words in the box to complete these statements.**

Adjective	Comparative	Superlative
good	better	best
bad	worse	worst

a)   The weather was terrible in Thailand! But we enjoyed Hong Kong because the weather was much .... there.

b)   It was a horrible flight across the Pacific. In fact, it was the .... flight I've ever had!

c)   The Park Hotel is a .... place to stay. It's not expensive, and the location is excellent.

d)   July is a .... month to travel in Europe than September. All the hotels are full, and the trains are very crowded.

e)   Hawaii has the .... beaches in the world. They are wonderful.

5 **Complete these facts using the superlative form of the adjectives.**

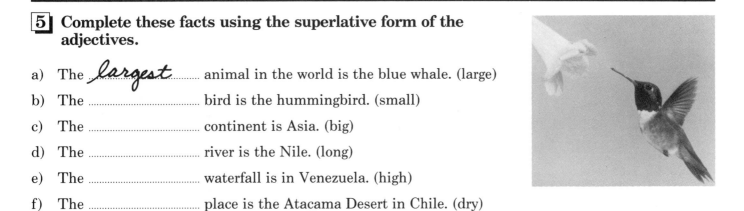

a) The *largest* animal in the world is the blue whale. (large)

b) The .... bird is the hummingbird. (small)

c) The .... continent is Asia. (big)

d) The .... river is the Nile. (long)

e) The .... waterfall is in Venezuela. (high)

f) The .... place is the Atacama Desert in Chile. (dry)

6 **Read about these countries. Find one thing wrong in each description.**

Australia is an island continent in the South Pacific. The capital is Canberra, but the city with the biggest population is Sydney, which has nearly four million. English is the first language of most people, but there are also many immigrants who speak other languages. Indonesia is one of Australia's nearest neighbors. It is only a short flight from the northern city of Darwin, Australia's biggest city.

Canada is the second largest country in land size. It stretches 3,223 miles from east to west, and from the North Pole to the U.S. border. Canada has a warm climate all year round. Both English and French are official languages. Many French-speaking people live in the province of Quebec, where Montreal is the biggest city. Canada has a cold winter, and many Canadians enjoy winter sports, such as skiing and ice skating.

Switzerland is a small country in central Europe. Its neighbors are France in the west, Italy in the south, Austria in the east, and Germany in the north. Sixty percent of the land is mountains. Switzerland is famous for its banks, tourism, and skiing. It's a very easy place to drive around because it's flat.

7 **Crossword puzzle: Did you know?**

Across clues

1 It doesn't cost much to stay at the YWCA. It's .... than a hotel.

3 Rome is .... in summer than Vienna. It's too hot for me.

4 The people are very nice here. They're .... than in my hometown.

5 Amsterdam is a beautiful .... city. There aren't many modern buildings.

9 The weather is terrible in the winter. It's .... in the summer.

10 There isn't much to see here. It's not an .... place to visit.

11 Which is the .... city in winter, Stockholm, Helsinki, or Berlin?

14 There's lots to do in New York. It's an .... city to visit.

15 There are a lot of people in Taipei. It's a .... city.

16 Vatican City is the .... country in the world. It has only 800 people.

Down clues

2 Japan is more .... than Hong Kong.

3 Your suitcase weighs 30 kilos. It's .... than mine.

4 I have never seen a city like Venice. It's very unusual. It's ....

6 The Pacific is larger than the Atlantic. It's the .... ocean in the world.

7 Mount Fuji is high, but it's not the .... mountain in the world.

8 San Francisco has unusual weather. It's .... in summer.

12 This place is not the same as my hometown. It's ....

13 I had a .... vacation. The weather was cold, and the hotel was expensive.

15 What are you doing Friday night?

1 **Complete this telephone conversation.**

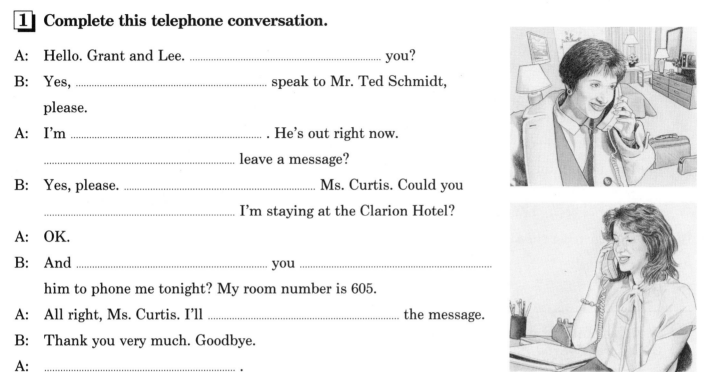

A: Hello. Grant and Lee. .... you?

B: Yes, ... speak to Mr. Ted Schmidt, please.

A: I'm .... He's out right now.

.... leave a message?

B: Yes, please. .... Ms. Curtis. Could you

.... I'm staying at the Clarion Hotel?

A: OK.

B: And .... you ....

him to phone me tonight? My room number is 605.

A: All right, Ms. Curtis. I'll .... the message.

B: Thank you very much. Goodbye.

A: ....

2 **Choose the correct response.**

a) Could you ask Rita
   to phone me?

   .... Good, thanks.

   .... OK. I'll tell her.

   .... Would you like to leave a message?

b) How about going to
   the football game
   on Sunday afternoon?

   .... No, I'm not.

   .... That's right.

   .... Sure. I'd love to.

c) Would you like to go
   to a movie on Saturday?

   .... Oh, sorry. I can't.

   .... Nothing special.

   .... Let's get together soon.

d) Let's get together
   soon.

   .... When would you like to come?

   .... That'd be nice.

   .... Yes, it would.

3 Put the words in the correct order.

A: Hello? Is Ann there?

B: No, she isn't. Do you want to leave a message?

A: Yes, thank you.

....

(Please   on   party   is   Fred   there
tell   Sunday   for   birthday   a   her)

B: Oh, OK.

A: .... ?

(And   at   tell   the   is   Jenny's   could
her   apartment   you   party)

B: All right. I'll tell her.

A: And one more thing.

....

(Please   her   bring   ask   guitar   her   to)

B: Sure. I'll give her the message.

A: Thanks. Bye!

B: Bye.

4 Which nouns go with which verbs? Write the nouns under the correct verbs.

have   read   see   take   visit   watch

an art gallery	a musical
a ballgame	a novel
a barbecue	a party
a cooking lesson	a picnic
a driving test	a play
a movie	a show
a museum	a video

5 Write invitations to four events in Hicksville using the patterns below.

THIS WEEK'S EVENTS IN HICKSVILLE	
Play	Tuesday night
Baseball game	Wednesday night
Art show	Friday night
Craft fair	Saturday
Tennis tournament	Sunday afternoon
Jazz concert	Sunday night

Would you like to go to a jazz concert on Sunday night?

(or)

There's a jazz concert on Sunday night. Would you like to go?

a) ....

b) ....

c) ....

d) ....

6 Write about your plans for Friday, Saturday, and Sunday like this.

I'm going to a business meeting on Friday morning. I'm having lunch with three co-workers at one o'clock. On Friday evening, I'm going to a concert with a friend from school.

Friday ....

Saturday ....

Sunday ....

59

7 Beyond the telephone

1 Read this passage with a dictionary. Then answer the questions below.

Remember, not so long ago, when the telephone used to be a simple receiver connected by a wire to the wall? And all you used your phone for was to make a phone call? Today, new technology has changed the telephone and what people use it for.

Computer-based technology has given us instant connections and clearer conversations over the telephone. Nowadays, people use telephones to do their banking, to rent videos, and to buy things. People use their telephones to connect their home computers to computerized information centers. People also send letters and documents through phone lines by fax. And new systems may be available shortly for sending video pictures over the telephone.

But you don't need to be at home or at the office to use the telephone anymore. Mobile phones (also known as cellular phones) have no wires. You can carry one in your pocket or keep one in your car. A call from a mobile phone travels along radio waves to stations located in different places. From there, the radio signal is connected to the regular phone system. With a mobile phone, anyone who can drive and talk can also drive and phone. This means less wasted time: You don't have to look for a phone booth or use coins to make a call. So remember, next time you are at the beach or riding your bicycle, there might be a call for you!

a) How have computers improved telephone services?

b) How many uses of the telephone can you find in the passage?

c) How many uses of a mobile phone can you find?

d) How does a mobile phone call reach a station?

2 How many different things do you use the telephone for?